This item should be returned to a Blackpool Library
on or before the latest date stamped below.

To extend the loan period please contact your local Library
or phone Central Renewals on (01253) 478070.

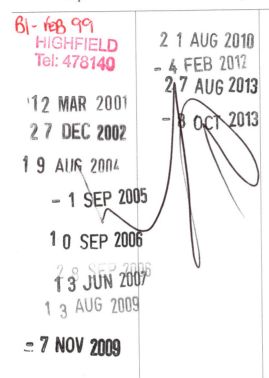

Russia

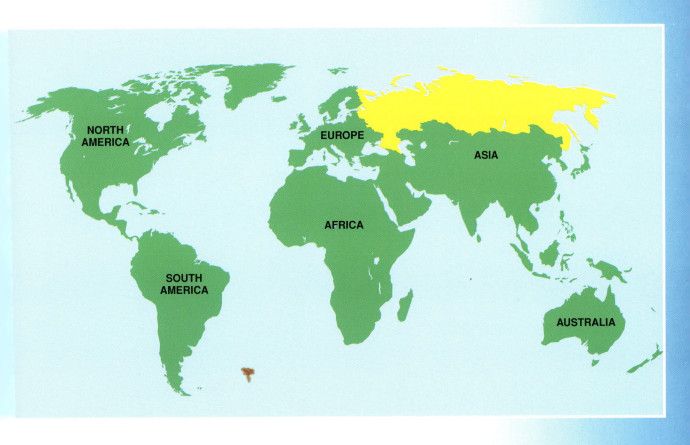

Fred Martin

First published in Great Britain by Heinemann Library
Halley Court, Jordan Hill, Oxford OX2 8EJ
a division of Reed Educational and Professional Publishing Ltd

OXFORD FLORENCE PRAGUE MADRID ATHENS
MELBOURNE AUCKLAND KUALA LUMPUR SINGAPORE TOKYO
IBADAN NAIROBI KAMPALA JOHANNESBURG GABORONE
PORTSMOUTH NH CHICAGO MEXICO CITY SAO PAULO

Designed by AMR
Illustrations by Art Construction
Printed and bound in Italy by L.E.G.O.

01 00 99 98 97
10 9 8 7 6 5 4 3 2 1

ISBN 0 431 01354 3

British Library Cataloguing in Publication Data

Martin, Fred, 1948-
Next Stop Russia
1. Russia (Federation) – Geography – Juvenile literature
I.Title II.Russia
914.7

Acknowledgements
The Publishers would like to thank the following for permission to reproduce photographs:
J. Allan Cash Ltd p.28; Colorific! D. Kampfner p.18, P. Turnley p.15; Robert Harding Picture Library P. Van Riel p.24, J. Shakespear p.29; Trip N. Gyngazov p.20, J. Heath p.23, M. Jenkin pp.4, 27, V. Kolpakov p.26, A. Kuznetsov p.9, V. Larionov p.22, N. Rudakov p.8, V. Sidoropolev p.14, A. Tjany-Rjadno pp.7, 12, 13, 16, 17, 19, 21, 25, B. Turner pp.5, 6, N. & J. Wiseman pp.10, 11.

Cover photograph reproduced with permission of Zefa Picture Library/Raga.

Our thanks to Chris Winter for his comments in the preparation of this book.

Every effort has been made to contact holders of any material reproduced in this book. Any omissions will be rectified in subsequent printings if notice is given to the Publisher.

CONTENTS

RUSSIA: PAST AND PRESENT

St Basil's cathedral in Moscow's Red Square.
*   *The cathedral was completed in 1560.*

Russian history

Russian history goes back well over 1000 years. At that time, the land was fought over by Khazars from Turkey, Vikings from Sweden and then Mongols from Asia. By 1300, Russia was a new country with its capital in Moscow. After that, land was captured on all sides and by 1649, Russia had extended to the Pacific Ocean.

Russia was ruled by powerful emperors called *tsars* [zars] from 1547 to 1917, when there was a revolution and the last tsar, Nicholas II, was put to death. By July 1923, many people had joined the revolution. They were attracted by the high ideals of sharing everything and all the people being equal. They called themselves the Union of Soviet Socialist Republics (USSR). This country was very much bigger than the original Russia. The **communist** party set itself up as a form of government under the leadership of Lenin. More land in Eastern Europe came under the control of the USSR after World War II.

The new Russia

In 1991, the communist government was forced to vote itself out of power, by public demand. The USSR broke up into separate countries. The biggest of these is the Russian Federation. Some parts of the USSR, such as Ukraine, have joined with the Russian Federation in a new group called the Commonwealth of Independent States (CIS).

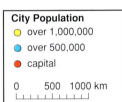
The Russian Federation stretches 10,000 kilometres from east to west and 5000 kilometres from north to south. It spans 11 time zones and is almost twice the size of the USA.

The communist government used to control all the factories, farms, shops, houses and people's jobs. Most people were not rich but everyone had a job and enough to eat. The leaders of the new Russian government want to make Russia more like **capitalist** countries such as the UK and USA. Business people can now own their own factories or shops and make money for themselves. However, many of the poorer people have found they are worse off.

The Russian Federation

The Russian Federation is the world's biggest country. It is divided into 21 self-governing **republics**, various territories, provinces and districts. There are about 150 million people in the Russian Federation. The people in the different republics are from different races, have different languages, traditions, religions and ways of life. Because of this, it is sometimes hard to get all the republics to work together.

The Russian flag.
- *The flag of the USSR was red with a gold hammer and sickle.*
- *Now the Russian flag has white, blue and red stripes with a crest of a two-headed eagle.*
- *This was the flag used by Tsar Peter the Great from 1694.*

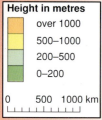

THE NATURAL LANDSCAPE

Height in metres
- over 1000
- 500–1000
- 200–500
- 0–200

0   500   1000 km

ARCTIC OCEAN

PACIFIC OCEAN

RUSSIA

Kamchatka Peninsula

R. Yenisey

R. Lena

R. Volga

Black Sea

Mt Elbrus 5633

Caucasus Mountains

Caspian Sea

Lake Baikal

Continental scale

Russia is so big that it spreads over part of two continents. The Ural Mountains divide Russia between Europe and Asia. In the north, along the **Arctic Circle**, you can travel almost half-way around the world and still be in Russia. Further east, Russia is separated from North America by the narrow Bering Strait.

There are large areas of **plains** where the land is mostly flat.

Land to the west of the Urals is part of the North European Plain that extends through Poland and Germany to the North Sea. The vast Siberian plains are divided in two by higher land named the Central Siberian **plateau**. Land in the south of Russia is called the **steppe**. The steppe used to be all grassland, but its black soil is among the most fertile in the world and much of it has been ploughed up for farming.

One of 22 active volcanoes on the Kamchatka Peninsula, in the far east of Russia.

- *Volcanic eruptions and earthquakes occur fairly often in this unstable area of the earth's surface.*

The widest bridge across the Volga.

- *The River Volga flows for 3700 kilometres south, from the Valdai hills north-west of Moscow to the Caspian Sea.*
- *About 200 main **tributaries** flow into the Volga.*

Russia's rivers and lakes

Some of the world's longest and widest rivers flow through Russia. Most flow north towards the Arctic Ocean. The Ob, the Yenisey and the Lena are three of the longest. In the west, the River Volga flows south for 3700 kilometres into the Caspian Sea. In spite of its name, the Caspian Sea is actually surrounded by land like a lake. It is the largest area of inland water in the world.

Mountains and hills

The rest of Russia's **physical geography** is made up of mountains and hills. The highest mountains are in the south-west where peaks rise to over 5000 metres. These are the Caucasus Mountains between the Black Sea and the Caspian Sea.

There are also mountains in the far east of Siberia and some of the most **active volcanoes** in the world on the Kamchatka **Peninsula**. This area is on the edge of the 'Pacific Ring of Fire' where volcanoes and **earthquakes** are common. Mount Klyuchevsk [kloo-CHEVsk] is the highest peak in the region and having erupted over 70 times since records began in 1967, is one of the world's most active volcanoes.

Lake Baikal in Siberia is the world's deepest lake at 1620 metres deep. It contains one-fifth of all the world's fresh water. At 25 million years old, it is also the oldest lake in the world.

CLIMATE, VEGETATION AND WILDLIFE

Murmansk, a port in the far north by the Arctic Ocean.

- *It is at **latitude** 69° north which is about $2\frac{1}{2}°$ north of the Arctic Circle.*
- *The average temperature is below freezing point for about 6 months.*
- *The sun never rises in January and December.*
- *The warmest month is July, with an average daily temperature of about 13°C.*

Extremes of temperature

Russia is so big that it contains many different climates. In the city of Irkutsk in Siberia, a winter temperature of –20°C is not uncommon and winter lasts for 9 months. North of the **Arctic Circle**, the temperature can be as low as –70°C. In Moscow, there are four months where the average temperature is below **freezing point**, but there is an average of 164 days of snow each year. In summer, the temperature rises to just over 20°C in Irkutsk and Moscow.

There are two main reasons why the temperatures are so different in different parts of Russia. One is that in the far north of Russia, the sun is always low in the sky. The little heat it gives is spread out over a large area so the ground stays cold. The second reason is that the central parts of Russia are up to 2000 kilometres from the nearest ocean. Mild air blowing off an ocean keeps the air warmer in winter and cooler in summer. Land away from the oceans becomes much colder in winter, but much warmer in summer.

From tundra to steppe

There are five broad bands of vegetation that change as the climate changes from north to south Russia. The far north inside the Arctic Circle is called the **tundra**. It is so cold that only mosses and lichens grow here. The soil is frozen in winter but in places the top 15 centimetres thaws out in summer and turns to marsh. South of the tundra, there is the **taiga**. This is a belt of **coniferous trees** which forms the largest area of forest in the world. Next, there is a wide band of **deciduous trees**. Further south, the trees are replaced by grasses in the **steppes**. Finally, the landscape changes to semi-desert at the southern borders.

Wildlife

Wild animals roam freely in places that are too cold or difficult for people to live in. There are polar bears and herds of reindeer in the tundra. Bears, wolves and elk live in the taiga forests. Wild boar and mink live in the deciduous forests. Other animals, such as polecats and jerboas, live in the steppes. There are only about 250 Siberian tigers left because so many have been hunted and shot. Their skin and bones are sold to be made into medicines and potions in some Asian countries.

More than half the total area of Russia has permafrost. This means that the ground is permanently frozen, to depths of up to hundreds of metres.

The taiga.
- *This is the wide band of coniferous forest that stretches across Russia.*
- *Large areas of the forest are being cut down to provide timber for industry.*

TOWNS AND CITIES

The old capital.
- *St Petersburg was Russia's capital city for about 200 years up to 1918.*
- *There are many canals and fine buildings in the city.*
- *St Petersburg was built in a marshy area where the River Neva flows into the sea.*
- *The city has been called Russia's 'window to the west'.*

Moscow

About three out of every four people in Russia live in towns and cities. The biggest cities are Moscow, with nine million people and St Petersburg, with over five million people. There are at least another 10 cities with a population of over a million.

Moscow is Russia's **capital city**. The centre of Moscow is a walled area known as the **Kremlin**. Red Square and St Basil's Cathedral are next to the Kremlin. Red Square is so called because the words for 'red' and 'beautiful' are the same in Russian.

The rest of Moscow spreads out in rings from the centre. There are industrial areas, parks and tall blocks of flats that spread out for about 50 kilometres from the centre.

You need an atlas that is up-to-date to find towns and cities in Russia. This is because many of them have changed their name, sometimes several times.

St Petersburg was changed to Petrograd, then to Leningrad before it changed back to St Petersburg in 1991.

St Petersburg

St Petersburg was built in 1703 by Peter the Great, considered by many to be the greatest of all Russia's tsars. He wanted a new capital city and a sea port with access to the rest of Europe. In 1905, outside the Tsar's Winter Palace in St Petersburg, troops fired at the crowd of men, women and children who were on a peaceful demonstration. This was one of the first revolts that led to Lenin's revolution in 1917. Like many other cities in the west of Russia, much of St Petersburg was destroyed during World War II. Fortunately, some of the finest buildings were saved and others have been restored.

Historic and working towns

North of Moscow, there is a 'Golden Ring' of cities, each with their own kremlin, cathedrals and other historic buildings. In Siberia, there are cities such as Irkutsk that grew on trading routes between Europe and China.

There are vast reserves of minerals such as coal, oil and metals in Russia, especially in Siberia. Towns such as Khabarovsk in the south-east have been built to provide a base for mining and for industry. There are very high levels of air **pollution** in some of these cities because of the industry.

A block of flats in Moscow.
- *Most Muscovites live in small apartments in tower blocks like these.*
- *Many people started moving to the towns and cities since the revolution in 1917.*

LIVING IN MOSCOW

The Oshurov's at home

Anatoly Oshurov, his wife Marina Oshurova and their daughter Anita live in Perovo, a suburb in the north of Moscow. They live in a small flat in an old apartment building with five floors. Most of the space in the small flat is taken up by chairs, tables and other furniture.

Anatoly working at his desk in his office.
- *Orders for his company's products are handled on computers.*
- *Anatoly usually works between 10.00 am and 6.00 pm.*

It is a pleasant area of the city where there are trees and open spaces. Most other Muscovites live in tall concrete blocks of flats that were built after World War II.

Jobs in new businesses

Anatoly works for a small company that sells fruit juice and milk. Many new private businesses have started up since the communist party rule came to an end in 1991.

Marina works for a company which helps people who want to emigrate and get married in other countries. Marina manages the advertising for the company. In the past, businesses did not advertise because they were all owned by the government, and very few people emigrated.

The block of flats where the Oshurov family live.
- *There is no lift to their fifth floor flat.*
- *Because so many people live in Moscow, space is short and there are very few individual houses.*

At school and home

Anita, aged twelve, is now going to secondary school. She is in class six in school N1125. They do not have school uniform, but the desks are always neatly arranged in straight rows. There is always homework to be done in the evening

Marina buys some food in the local shops but likes to buy fresh vegetables in the market. The family's favourite meals are Russian salad, *borsch*, (which is beetroot soup) and *blinis*, (small pancakes).

The cost of most things in the shops has gone up in recent years. The Oshurov family hope that this will change. They look forward to a time when there will be better wages and the prices of goods will not go up so quickly.

Anita in her classroom in school N1125.
- *Anita wants to study foreign languages to help her get a job.*

The Oshurov family eating their evening meal in the kitchen.
- *The family have a balanced diet including vegetables and fruit.*

FARMING LANDSCAPES

Combine harvesters harvesting wheat in the south-west of Russia.
- *Only the large state farms could afford combine harvesters.*
- *Wheat grows well in the warm summer climate of this area.*

A lack of farmland

There are 150 million people to feed in Russia. Most of the food has to be grown in Russia, because buying it in from other countries is too expensive. Unfortunately, much of Russia is not suitable for farming. It is either too cold, too steep and high, or the soil is too poor. Also, the climate makes farming very difficult. This is why there are sometimes shortages of some types of food.

Farms until 1991

Until 1991, almost all the farmland in Russia was owned and run by the government. There were huge farms called *sovhozs* [SOV-hots] where people worked for low wages. They produced what the government said they had to grow. There were also state **collective** farms called *kolhozs* [kol-HOTS] where people could take some share in the profits. Such profits were never high because the government set all the prices for food to make sure that everyone could have a basic diet at a low cost.

Farms since 1991

Since 1991, the old way of running farms has started to change. The state still owns and runs a lot of farms, but others are owned by individuals who make their own decisions and take their own profits. Prices in the shops are no longer restricted so farmers are able to make greater profits. This is causing problems for many Russian people because fresh fruit and vegetables have become very expensive.

The type of farming in Russia depends on the climate in each area. The warmer areas in the south-west are best for **arable** crops such as wheat, rye and maize. There are more cattle further north where it is wetter and a bit cooler. Vegetables are grown near towns and cities. Some farmers now bring their vegetables and other produce to street markets in the cities. They sell what they have produced for the highest price they can get.

Only 8% of Russian land is used for growing crops. About 6% is used for growing grass for grazing.

Russian soldiers helping to bring in a crop of potatoes from fields near Moscow.
- *Potatoes are one of the main foods eaten in Russia.*

A FARMING FAMILY IN RUSSIA

The Dmitreiev's house in the village of Protasova Orlovskaya.
- *There is enough land for them to grow their own vegetables.*

The Dmitreiev family

Sergey Dmitreiev, his wife Olga Dmitreieeva and their two children Andrey and Misha, live in a village about 300 km south of Moscow. Sergey is 32 years old, Olga is 27, their son is nine and their daughter Misha is two.

The family house is a one-storey building that has four rooms and a big kitchen. They have more space than most people who live in the cities. They are not a rich family but they do have a TV, a stereo and a washing machine.

Making a living

Sergey and Olga both work on a co-operative farm. About 100 people work on the farm. Most people in this part of Russia depend on farming for their living. It is a fertile area where crops such as wheat are grown. There are dairy herds producing milk. Pigs and horses are also reared on the farm.

Sergey works on a farm driving a tractor and doing other jobs.
- *The farm is a co-operative that the village people all own and help to run.*

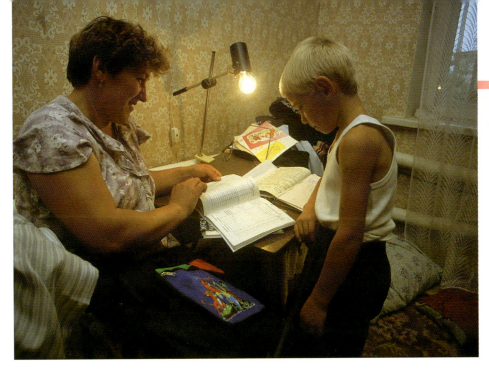

Olga helps her son Andrey with his homework at night.

- *She is keen for him to do well at school so that he can get a good job when he is older.*

Sergey's job is to drive a tractor and a combine harvester. He also works with the cattle. Olga works as a milkmaid. They work for up to 12 hours each day for most of the year. However, during the depths of winter, nothing can be done in the fields.

They also have a garden where they grow flowers and most of the vegetables they need. They grow cabbages, tomatoes, cucumbers, beetroot and apples. Other food such as bread and meat is bought at the local village shop.

School and leisure

Andrey walks to the local village school every day. It is only five minutes away. This year he is in class three with 15 other children. His school subjects include maths, history, geography and the Russian language and literature. His mother often helps him with his homework.

Andrey has some toy cars and tractors but his favourite game is playing football with the other village children. The family work together in their garden. When they have time, they go for a walk in the country.

Living and growing up in Russia's countryside is hard work, but Andrey has already decided that he wants to stay in the countryside when he grows up. Perhaps Misha will do the same, or perhaps she will move to a city for work.

WHAT'S IN RUSSIAN SHOPS?

Times of change

Before 1991, under the **communist** government, there were always enough basic foods such as bread and potatoes. But there were often shortages of meat, dairy foods and fresh vegetables. Other goods, such as clothes and shoes, were also expensive and hard to find. People had a very limited choice of cars and few could afford to run them.

Since 1991, some people have started to open their own shops and businesses. Supermarkets are opening in many of Moscow's **suburbs**, but there are still shortages of many goods. This could change if Russians produced more goods to **export**. Profits made from such exports could be used to **import** more shortage goods from other countries. The money could also be used to make more goods in Russia.

Already, more goods from other countries are coming into Russia. These include BMW cars from Germany and Cadillacs from the USA. They remain luxury items, and can only be bought by the few people who have become very rich in the new Russia.

A shopping arcade in Moscow.
- *Some people in the new Russia have become very rich.*
- *Expensive goods made in Russia or bought in from other countries, are now being sold in some Moscow shops.*

Moscow street stalls.
- *Farmers bring food to be sold for the best price they can get.*
- *Some people are now so poor that they have to sell the last of their possessions.*

Markets and stores

There are many small kiosks in the streets, where people buy their newspapers and other small items. Food is usually bought in a street market. Farmers and other small business owners are now selling goods in markets rather than through shops because they can charge higher prices by doing this. Because of the increased prices, people without much money, especially the elderly, are finding it harder to buy the food and other basic goods they need.

Lots of new shops are opening in Moscow and St Petersburg. These include new Russian stores as well as international shops such as Benetton, Littlewoods and Gucci. The GUM arcade is one of the busiest places to shop in Moscow. In Russian, the letters spell out the State Universal Store. The arcade has shops that sell all sorts of goods, including expensive furs and other clothes.

Russian gifts

There are shops in most cities where Russians and visitors from other countries can buy souvenirs and other luxury goods. A favourite gift from Russia is a set of *Matryoshka* dolls. These are rounded hollow wooden figures that are brightly painted. Each doll fits inside another doll.

Many Russians are keen chocolate eaters. Chocolate lovers in St Petersburg will be pleased to hear that Cadbury Schweppes have plans to build a new chocolate factory close to their city.

RUSSIAN FOOD AND COOKING

A group of friends are having a barbecue in the country.
- *The fur hats and vodka help to keep people warm.*

Traditional foods

Most Russians eat a basic diet because of seasonal shortages and a lack of affordable food. There are special dishes in each part of Russia, but buying the ingredients to make them is not always easy. Fresh meat is especially expensive.

Foods such as beetroot soup called *borsch*, cabbage soup called *shchi*, potatoes and small pancakes called *blinis,* are often eaten. A porridge named *kasha* which is made from buckwheat is eaten for breakfast. Processed meat such as sausages and different types of fish or chicken are often eaten as a main meal.

The world's largest MacDonald's hamburger restaurant is now in Moscow. Many Russian people do not want to eat this type of American 'fast food'. Others feel that it is a sign that their standard of living is improving.

Traditional drinks

Tea is drunk without milk or sugar. The traditional way to make tea is to heat the water on a charcoal burner called a *samovar*. *Kvas* is a drink made from rye bread mixed with jam or honey and yeast. Vodka is a strong and cheap alcoholic drink which is made from potatoes. It is drunk both in bars and at home.

Meat dishes and caviar

Beef *strogonov* is a traditional Russian dish. Strips of beef steak are fried and then put in a casserole with sour cream, onions, mushrooms and other vegetables. There are many types of chicken dish such as chicken *kiev*, named after the city of Kiev, as well as dishes that use duck and lamb.

Caviar is one of the best-known foods from Russia. Black caviar is the eggs from a fish called a sturgeon. The most expensive caviar comes from the Beluga sturgeon that lives in the Caspian Sea. There is also red caviar that comes from salmon.

A family meal in a country area of Russia.
- *The family grow many of their own vegetables in their garden.*
- *Sausages, soup, bread and some vegetables are eaten for the family's evening meal.*

MADE IN RUSSIA

Tractors waiting to be delivered at a factory.
- *These tractors will be used in the timber industry.*
- *Timber, which is sold to other countries, provides a valuable income.*

Satellites and space

The first satellite to orbit the Earth was launched by the USSR in 1957. In 1961, the USSR was also the first country to launch a man, Yuri Gagarin, into space. The Russian words *sputnik* (satellite) and *cosmonaut* (astronaut) are now part of the English language. These successes showed the world that the USSR was a modern industrial country in space technology.

New thinking

Russia has metals such as iron ore and copper, as well as sources of energy, such as oil and natural gas. However, most of these resources are in Siberia where the freezing winter climate makes working there very difficult. It is also difficult to transport the resources to factories.

Russia has run out of money to spend on its satellites and space research. By 1995, some Russian space scientists were working on computer games instead!

A metal smelting factory.
- *These provide raw materials for Russia's industries.*
- *Factories such as these can cause enormous air and water pollution.*
- *Piles of waste rock make a spoil tip.*

The new government is trying to change the kind of goods being made in Russia. Fewer tanks and other weapons are being produced. Instead, there are factories making **consumer goods**, like microwaves or washing machines, that people want in their homes. Also, many of these goods are **exported** and this helps bring more money into Russia.

Goods can be made cheaply in Russia, partly because workers' wages are much lower than in countries such as the UK. In time, Russian workers should start to earn higher wages and be able to afford a more 'western' standard of living.

Environmental care

The environment in most of Russia's industrial areas has become very **polluted**. Air pollution and water pollution from factories make it unhealthy for people who live there. Breathing problems such as asthma are common. More serious diseases have been caused by lead and by leaks from nuclear power stations. Taking more care of the environment is one aim of the new Russian government.

The station at Irkutsk in Siberia.

- *The Trans-Siberian express train runs through Irkutsk.*
- *The train is the best way for most people to travel long distances in Russia.*

Time to go

Travel between different places in Russia can be a problem. The country's size and harsh climate are two reasons for this. Travelling across Russia takes you through eleven **time zones**, (there is one hour's difference between each zone). This means that in the morning, while people are going to work in Vladivostock on the Pacific coast, it is still midnight in Moscow!

The Trans-Siberian railway and the Baikal-Amur railway cross Siberia to link Russia from east to west. The Trans-Siberian train from Moscow to Vladivostock has given better access to the mineral wealth and settlements along its route. Most of the railway lines in Russia are used for carrying heavy **freight** and food.

The main Russian airline is Aeroflot. Flying is the quickest but most expensive way to travel. A flight from Moscow to Irkutsk in central Siberia takes seven hours. This is about the same time it takes for a **sub-sonic** aircraft to cross from London to Washington in America.

The Trans-Siberian railway line is the longest in the world. It runs for 9310 kilometres, makes 92 stops and takes just over a week to complete its journey.

City travel

Not many people in Russia own their own car because cars and petrol are too expensive. People rely on **public transport** and taxis to get about in towns and cities. Public transport, such as buses and underground rail services, is cheap and efficient.

The Moscow Underground (Metro) was opened in 1935. Some of the Metro stations have marble columns, mosaics and hanging chandeliers. They are all kept spotlessly clean. Travelling around Moscow by Metro is quicker and cheaper than going by car.

Roads and rivers

Most of the best roads in Russia are in the west. Very little freight is carried in lorries because the roads are generally so poor and the distances are so great. Roads in the coldest parts of Russia cannot be used in winter because of thick snow. But Russians do build their vehicles to start up when the temperature is below **freezing point**.

Rivers and canals are used by passengers and for freight. The problem again is that the rivers freeze over in winter. In Siberia, cars and lorries sometimes use the frozen rivers as roads.

An escalator taking passengers to an underground Metro station in Moscow.
- *Most people in Moscow travel by public transport.*

25

LEISURE AND SPORT

Russian recreation

Summer or winter, there is always something for people in Russia to do in their spare time. In the cities, there are centres for sports such as ice-skating and swimming. In winter, the lakes in St Petersburg's Central Recreation Park are frozen so people are able to skate on them. Visiting the Turkish baths or saunas is also a popular way of relaxing. More people are now playing sports such as golf and tennis, although these are very expensive.

People from the cities sometimes stay in country houses called *dachas* at weekends. Many townspeople still have relatives in the country who live in these small houses.

They grow vegetables on small plots beside the *dacha* which they take back to the cities to eat. A few of the wealthier Russians also have holiday apartments in Europe.

Sporting Russia

Russian governments have always spent money on providing good sports facilities and training. Russian gymnasts, athletes and ice-skaters are trained to the highest international standards and often win gold medals at international sporting events.

Football and ice hockey are popular spectator sports. The Moscow Dynamo football club is well known in international competitions.

Reindeer racing in the northern city of Murmansk.
- *The cold does not stop Russians enjoying outdoor sports.*
- *Other competitions include swimming in sub-zero temperatures!*

A small wooden house in the country called a dacha.

- *Some Russian people who live in cities own a dacha.*
- *They visit the dacha at weekends or for holidays.*

Tourist Russia

Since 1991, the number of tourists visiting Russia has increased. New facilities and places to stay are being built for the visitors. At Star City near Moscow, visitors will be able to learn about the cosmonauts' way of life. Resorts on the Black Sea, such as Dagomys, are being opened up to foreign tourists. As some ordinary people in Russia are becoming richer and have greater freedom to travel, they are making use of these leisure facilities as well.

Large areas of Russia are still unspoilt and have beautiful scenery and some exciting wildlife to see. Tour operators in Russia now offer adventure holidays in Siberia that include rafting, hunting and fishing.

In the 1996 Olympics in Atlanta, USA, Russian athletes won 26 gold medals. They were second only to the USA in the total number of gold medals they won.

CUSTOMS AND ARTS

An Easter procession held by the Russian Orthodox Church.
• *Many of the older people kept their religious beliefs during the communist years.*

May Day

On 1 May, Russians celebrate International Solidarity Day. This reminds Russian workers that they are working together for the same cause. Before 1991, it was also a spectacular display of military strength with troops, tanks, guns and missiles being paraded through Red Square. Now the parade is mainly to show the peaceful things that are done in Russia.

Religious festivals

The **communist** government prevented people from taking part in religious activities. In spite of this, many people continued to belong to their different faiths. Now that the communist government is gone, more people are joining the different religious groups and taking part in religious festivals again.

Christmas is one of the main events in the year. For Russian Orthodox Christians, Christmas is celebrated on 7 February. This is because the calendar of the Russian Orthodox Church is different to ours.

Art and architecture

The statues and monuments to famous communists, such as Lenin and Marx, are enormous and striking objects. They can be found all over Russia. Some have been defaced or destroyed in recent years. Those that remain, especially the huge buildings, are reminders of Russia's recent past.

This conversation from the Internet describes what one Russian ship's captain thinks of classical music: 'I don't like it. What kind of music do I like? Honestly? Really honestly? Deep Purple, Black Sabbath, Led Zeppelin, Ozzy Osbourne. Ozzy Osbourne is great'.

Some of the finest Russian art is religious. Small paintings called icons are holy objects as well as being art treasures. The great cathedrals, such as St Basil's cathedral in Moscow, with such distinctive skylines, date from the 16th century. The Hermitage is the largest public museum and art gallery in Russia, and is one of the most important collections in the world. Built in the 18th century for Catherine the Great, today it holds ancient and modern art from all corners of the earth.

The arts

Russian people have a great love of the arts such as ballet, music and literature. Many famous composers come from Russia, such as Tchaikovsky [chy-KOVsky] and Stravinsky. Famous writers such as Tolstoy, Dostoyevsky and Chekhov came from Russia. The Bolshoi ballet Company from Moscow and the Moscow State Circus perform all over the world.

There are different musical and folk-dancing traditions in different parts of Russia. Cossack dancing is well known for its muscular and energetic performances. There is now a folk theatre in St Petersburg where music and dancing from different places in Russia are performed. This helps preserve the customs and provides entertainment for Russian people and tourists.

This parade in Moscow celebrates Victory Day.
- *War veterans are marching to remind people of the end of World War II in Europe.*
- *The parade is held on 9 May every year.*
- *Some people are holding the old USSR flag.*

RUSSIA FACTFILE

Area 17,075,400 square kilometres

Highest point Mount Elbrus 5633 m

Climate

	January temp.	July temp.	Total annual rainfall
Moscow	–10°C	20°C	575 mm

Population 150 million

Population density 9 people per square kilometre

Life expectancy
Female 74
Male 64

Capital city Moscow

Population of the main cities (in millions)

Moscow	9.0
St Petersburg	5.0
Nizhniy Novgorod	1.5
Novosibirsk	1.5
Yekaterinburg	1.4

Land use

Forest	45%
Other	41%
Farming	8%
Grass	6%

Employment

Industry	46%
Services	34%
Farming	20%

Main imports
Machinery and transport equipment
Food
Manufactured goods
Chemicals

Main exports
Mineral fuels and raw materials
Machinery and transport equipment
Crude materials
Manufactured goods

Language

Russian	87%
Tartar	3%
Ukranian	1%
Chuvash	1%
Other	8%

Religions
Christianity
Islam
Buddhism

Money
1 rouble = 100 kopecks

Wealth $2350
(The total value of what is produced by the country in one year, divided by its population and converted into US dollars).

GLOSSARY

active volcano volcano that is still likely to erupt

arable a type of farming which refers specifically to plant crops

Arctic Circle an imaginary line around the north polar regions

capital city the city where a country has its government

capitalist a political system that allows people to own businesses and make profits

collective a system in which people work together for their material benefit, rather than compete against each other

communist communists believe that all property, especially land and businesses, should be owned by the state on behalf of all the country's people

coniferous trees trees with needle-like leaves and cones

consumer goods goods made for people to buy in shops

deciduous trees trees that shed their leaves at the end of the growing season

earthquake violent shaking of the ground

exports goods sent out of a country to be sold to other countries

freezing point 0°C, the point at which water becomes frozen

freight goods transported in containers

imports goods brought into a country to be sold there

kremlin the walled fortress found around many old Russian towns and cities

latitude an imaginary line of measurement around the Earth which runs parallel to the Equator

peninsula a long area of land that is surrounded on three sides by the sea

physical geography the shape of the land, and the rivers, soils, climate and natural vegetation found on it

plains large areas of mainly flat land

plateau flat-topped upland area surrounded by steep slopes

pollution different ways in which the air, water or ground are made dirty

public transport a type of transport that anyone can use and that is set up by the government

republic a country ruled by a government, that does not have a king or a queen

steppe the name given to plains in the south of Russia

sub-sonic speeds less than the speed of sound

suburb an area on the outskirts of a city, usually residential

taiga the name in Russia given to the large areas of coniferous forest

time zone the world is divided into 24 time zones, each one is an hour different in time from the zone either side of it

tributaries a smaller river that joins a larger one

tundra a very cold landscape where little can grow

INDEX